Contents

KU-655-494

Introduction

WHAT IS TIME?

Can you tell me the time? What's today's date? When was Abraham Lincoln born? What time is the big game on TV? How far away are the stars? These are all questions about time. We use time in many ways – when we look at a clock, consult a calendar or timetable, look up a history date, check a diary or the TV listings.

PEOPLE AND TIME

For most of the thousands of years that people have lived on Earth, they measured time by the daily rising and setting of the Sun. Today, most people live by clock-time. We get up, have breakfast, catch a bus, go to school 'on time' and we try not to be 'late'. Eventually, it's bedtime. Another day has passed. As time passes, we get older. We grow up, and our bodies change because all living things have body clocks too.

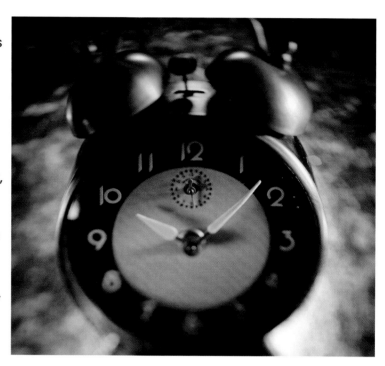

Many clocks, like this alarm clock, show 12 hours. The longer minute pointer moves 12 times faster than the hour pointer. On a 24-hour digital clock the time here could be shown as 10.07 (a.m.) or 22.07 (p.m.).

PRESENT, PAST AND FUTURE

'Now' – the time it takes you to read these words – is what we call the present. We look forward to a time we do not yet know: to the weekend, to holidays, to our next birthday. We call this the future. We can 'visit' the past through what we and other people remember, as well as through books, films, photographs, paintings, old buildings and antiques.

Time seems to flow, like a river. We can draw time-lines to show how one event (for example, the battle of Hastings in 1066) came so many years before another (the first landing on the Moon in 1969, for instance). We divide time into centuries, ages and eras, yet time still remains puzzling as it is not constant.

ABOUT TIME

Measuring Time

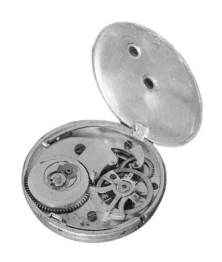

Brian Williams

CHERRYTREE BOOKS

Published by CHERRYTREE PRESS
327 High Street
Slough
Berkshire
SL1 1TX

Created and designed by
THE FOUNDRY DESIGN AND PRODUCTION
Crabtree Hall, Crabtree Lane, Fulham, London, SW6 6TY

Special thanks to Lucy Bradbury, Vicky Garrard and the late Helen Courtney

British Library Cataloguing in Publication data.
Williams, Brian, 1943 Oct. 7-
Measuring time. - (About time)
1.Time measurements - Juvenile literature
I.Title
526.7
ISBN 18234126X

First published 2002

Printed in Hong Kong by Wing King Tong Co. Ltd

Acknowledgements

The author and publishers would like to thank the following for permission to reproduce Photographs: Front cover and Title page Photodisc, Inc, Foundry Arts and Science Museum/ Science & Society Picture Library page 4 Photodisc, Inc page 5 (top) Warren Faidley/Int'l Stock/Robert Harding Picture Library (bottom) Private Collection/Bridgeman Art Library page 6 (top) Musee Conde, Chantilly, France/ Bridgeman Art Library (bottom) Kevin Johnson/Science & Society Picture Library page 7 John Sanford/Science Photo Library page 8 (top) Bonhams, London/Bridgeman Art Library (bottom) Science Museum/Science & Society Picture Library page 9 Foundry Arts page 10 (top) Royal Geographical Society /Bridgeman Art Library (bottom) Science Museum/Science & Society Picture Library page 11 Science Museum/Science & Society Picture Library page 12 (top) Index/Bridgeman Art Library (bottom) Robert H R.Frerck/Robert Harding Picture Library page 13 Science Museum/Science & Society Picture Library page 14 (top) Salisbury Cathedral, Wiltshire/Bridgeman Art Library (bottom) Topham Picturepoint page 15 Karen Villabona page 16 (top) Science Museum/Science & Society (bottom) Christie's Images page 17 Science Museum/Science & Society picture Library page 18 (top) The British Art Library (bottom) Bridgeman Art Library page 19 Science Museum/Science & Society Picture Library page 20 Peter Willi/Bridgeman Art Library page 21 (all) Science Museum/Science & Society Picture Library page 22(top) Petworth House, West Sussex /Bridgeman Art Library (bottom) John Bethell/Bridgeman Art Library page 23 Science Museum/Science & Society Picture Library page 24 (top) Topham Picturepoint (bottom) Science Museum/Science & Society Picture Library page 25 Robert Harding Picture Library page 26 (top) Fritz Polking/Still Pictures (bottom) Still Pictures page 27 Topham Picturepoint page 28 Topham Picturepoint page 29 (top) Jacobs/Robert Harding Picture Library (bottom) Ronald Grant Archive

SPACE TIME AND HUMAN TIME

Nothing in the Universe seems to stand still. The Sun is a star, and stars are born and grow old. The Universe appears to be getting bigger all the time. Thinking about 'space-time' is difficult, especially as the numbers are so big. Scientists measure star-distances not in miles or kilometres, but in light-years, the time it takes light to travel to Earth from far-distant stars. When we look at those stars, we are looking back in time, to what the stars were like when the light left them.

A millennium in history (1,000 years) seems a very long time to us, but in the Universe, it is the briefest moment.

There are probably billions of galaxies or star-systems. Even travelling at light-speed, it would take 150,000 years to reach the galaxy closest to our own Milky Way galaxy. Some giant galaxies are half a million light-years across.

MAKING SENSE OF TIME

From the earliest times, people were aware of time. They watched the seasons change, and the Sun rise and set. Prehistoric hunters did not need to measure anything smaller than a day. About 5,000 years ago, when hunters settled down to become farmers, they lived in towns and traded with their neighbours, so time began to matter. That is when people first made clocks.

Measuring time helped people to make sense of the world, as well as to regulate their lives. Scientists used time-measuring to investigate how the world worked.

With the Industrial Revolution and the dawn of the factory age in the nineteenth century, everyday life became ruled by time. The old rhythms of life were replaced by the fast ticking of clocks. Now we can measure time in tiny fractions of a second – yet we feel like we have less and less of it!

An 18th-century garden sundial. For thousands of years, people have used sundials to measure time, watching the shadow of a pointer move around a dial.

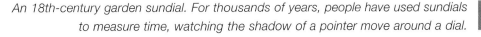

Moon Time

SILVER MOON, GOLDEN SUN

The new Moon hangs like a silver crescent in the night sky. It appears roughly every 29 days. People have noted its arrival ever since prehistoric times, when humans gazed at the Moon from the darkness of their caves.

The Moon and Sun were the earliest universal 'measurers of time'. They were the twin rulers: Night and Day, Dark and Light. In many ancient religions, the Moon was a mighty god or goddess, almost as powerful as the Sun.

It was simple to count time in 'moons'. By studying the Moon's face in its cycle of changes, from new to full, the Ancient Babylonians of Mesopotamia counted 'months' and also years. They made moon-calendars. However, moon-calendars proved unreliable: they did not keep step with the changing seasons. The Sun gave a more accurate time-guide.

A sailors' direction-finder (from Britanny, France 1546) showing the points of the compass and the phases of the Moon. Breton seamen would have used this calendar-chart to help plot a course between ports.

TRUE TO THE MOON

The Ancient Egyptians followed the Sun for their calendar. The Babylonians stuck with the Moon, mightiest of their sky gods, and their astrologer-priests

were able to predict eclipses – those startling moments when the Moon hides the Sun or when the Moon itself is blotted out by the Earth's shadow. Babylon's mathematicians struggled to match Moon-time with Sun-time, but by doing the complicated sums brought about useful advances in mathematics. However, they did not quite solve the problem.

The Moon gives off no light of its own. It 'shines' because it reflects light from the Sun. When the Moon moves between the Earth and the Sun it looks dark – sunlight can reach only the side facing away from us.

An eclipse of the Sun, showing the 'diamond ring' effect as the Moon hides the Sun's bright disc. A total eclipse blots out the Sun, turning day into night as the Moon's shadow passes across the Earth.

HOW OLD ARE MOON ROCKS?

The Moon may be as old as the Earth, about 4,600 million years. But astronauts who visited the Moon on the Apollo spacecraft, between 1969 and 1972, found no Moon rocks older than 4,200 million years.

This is what we call a new Moon. As the Moon moves around the Earth, the Sun lights up more of the side facing towards us, until a full Moon is seen. The Moon then wanes, or grows smaller, again.

The period from one new Moon to the next (called a 'synodic month') lasts about 29.5 days. The changing faces that we see are the phases of the Moon.

There is another moon-month, called the sidereal, or 'star', month. It lasts 27.3 days, which is the time it takes the Moon to orbit the Earth once. It is measured by lining up the Moon with a certain star and counting the days until the Moon returns to the same position. The sidereal month is shorter than the synodic month because of the way the Earth moves at the same time, in its path around the Sun.

The phases of the Moon. Gradually the Moon 'lights up' from new to full, then is once more shadowed by the Earth.

MOON CALENDARS

Many people in the ancient world used the Moon to fix the time of magical ceremonies and religious festivals. Jews and Muslims still follow a Moon-based calendar.

Muslims watch the Moon to find the dates for the pilgrimage to Mecca and for the fasting month of Ramadan. In each year, these important religious events take place about 10 days earlier than in the previous year. The date of the Christian festival of Easter is also tied to the cycles of the Moon.

KEY DATES

▶ **2200 BC** People in Mesopotamia study eclipses of the Moon; Babylonian astrologers predict eclipses – a useful trick for fortune-tellers!

▶ **459 BC** A Greek scientist named Anaxogoras realises that eclipses are caused by the Earth blocking sunlight reaching the Moon, and that the Moon gives no light of its own

▶ **350 BC** Another Greek, Aristotle, points out that the curved edge of an eclipse-shadow on the Moon proves that the Earth is a sphere

▶ **150 BC** Greek scientists measure how long it takes for the Moon to orbit the Earth (the synodic month); they also discover that the Moon affects the ocean tides

Sun Time

LIGHT AND DARK

Imagine you live any time before 200 years ago. There is no electric light, only flickering oil lamps and candles. When the Sun sets, darkness shrouds the world. Each dawn, light returns. What a relief! No wonder people were glad when the Sun banished darkness, and welcomed the new day.

Many peoples of the ancient world worshipped a Sun-god. To explain the movement of the Sun, the Greeks told how the god Apollo drove his golden chariot across the heavens every day. Other peoples had similar stories to explain the Sun's daily journey across the sky from east to west.

The Sun-god Apollo rode across the heavens, banishing the dark clouds of night. This 18th-century painting honours the Hapsburg emperor Charles VI, by showing him as Apollo in his dazzling chariot.

SHADOW CLOCKS

The Sun can be used as a clock. A shadow cast by the Sun gets shorter as the Sun rises higher. Watching shadows thrown by a stick or a stone gave someone the idea for making a shadow-clock, or sundial. The Egyptians were using shadow-clocks more than 3,500 years ago. So were people in Mesopotamia.

The simplest sundial is a stick stuck into the sand, which is used as a pointer. The length and angle of the stick's shadow changes as the Sun moves across the sky during the day. By drawing lines in the sand around the stick, people could 'tell the time' by seeing which line the shadow had reached. They made more lasting sundials from clay and stone, in which scratched marks around the pointer showed 'hours'.

The Ancient Egyptians used shadow-clocks such as this one, some 3,000 years old. The board was placed to lie east-west so that the pins cast shadows to record the passing hours.

STONEHENGE SUN-CLOCK

All over the world there are temples and other monuments linked to Sun-worship and time-measuring. Stonehenge in England is a circle of huge stones, set up about 5,000 years ago. People came to Stonehenge to celebrate the summer solstice – midsummer day, the longest day of the year. The stones were placed with care so that astronomer-priests could watch the Sun and fix the time for the important ceremony.

NO SUN, NO TIME

The Greeks and Romans also relied on sundials, even for fixing meal-times. The Romans used 13 different kinds of sundials. But sundials were not ideal for keeping time: to start with they do not work on cloudy days. Also, sundial hours and sundial days are different lengths in different places.

A sundial is most accurate near the equator, where the Sun is overhead, meaning that all the hours are roughly the same length. But in northern Europe, a summer hour is longer than a winter hour! Still people managed, for even in the well-run Roman Empire, minute-by-minute time-keeping did not yet matter. Roman time could even be stretched! The priests were in charge of the old Roman calendar; they decided when one year ended and a new year began. By making a year extra long, they could let politician-friends hold their jobs for a few days longer!

The biggest sun-clocks were obelisks like this, set up in public places in Egypt and Rome. They worked on the same principle as the sundial. The shadow pointed to the time (in hours).

KEY DATES

▶ **5000 BC** Egyptians and Babylonians use sundials
▶ **2950 BC** Work starts on building Stonehenge
▶ **300 BC** Romans divide the day into two parts: before midday (*ante meridiem*, or a.m.) and after midday (*post meridiem*, or p.m.); we still use these abbreviations today
▶ **100 BC** Romans have sundials in town squares; some Romans also carry pocket sundials
▶ **44 BC** Julius Caesar reforms the Roman calendar so that it has a regular year of 12 months

Marking the Day

MEASURING THE WORLD

As early as the 400s BC, the Greeks realised that the Earth was round, not flat. In the late 200s BC Eratosthenes, a clever Greek who lived in north Africa, worked out how to measure the distance around the Earth. He did this by watching shadows cast by the Sun.

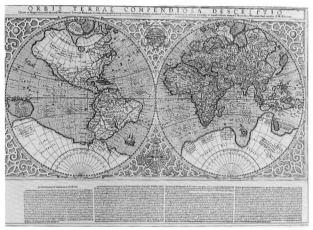

By this time, mathematicians knew that a sphere could be split into equal-sized segments, like pieces of an orange. In the second century AD, a Greek geographer named Ptolemy mapped the world into pieces, or zones, by day-length and climate. His map showed only the world the Greeks knew (mainly Europe and parts of Africa and Asia), and was not very accurate. But it was a start.

▲ *Even in the AD 1500s, geographers still relied heavily on the old maps of the Greeks, but were able to add new continents. This sixteenth-century German world map shows North and South America.*

WATER-CLOCKS

As cities grew, trade developed, and life became busier. Wandering hunters had not needed clocks, but city merchants and government officials did, as did priests, to ensure temple ceremonies were held at the proper times. To keep time at night, and on cloudy days when sundials did not work, inventors made water-clocks, and these were used in homes and temples.

A water-clock measures drips. An Ancient Egyptian water-clock was a clay pot with a small hole near the bottom, and a scale marked on the inside. The pot was filled with water, and as the water dripped out, people looked at the mark closest to the water level to see the time.

Another, more advanced water-clock measured time as water flowed from one pot into another. Here the water-level rose up the scale. An Egyptian 'summer night' measured '12 fingers' of water. A 'winter night' was longer, '14 fingers'.

A modern plaster copy of a water-clock from Karnak in Egypt. It was made around 1400 BC from a mineral called alabaster, and had a single drip-hole.

CUT OFF IN MID-DRIP

Water-clocks were used to time Roman lawyers in court. A lawyer might ask for six water-clocks to make his speech. If he ran out of arguments, he could cut the speech short by drinking the water from one or more of his clocks!

Most water-clocks ran dry in 20 minutes and had to be refilled by slaves, so it was not a very reliable way of keeping time. People spoke of 'losing water' when they meant 'wasting time'.

CANDLES AND RUNNING SAND

Ancient clock-watchers had two other useful time-keepers: candle clocks and sand-glasses – the kind people still use as egg-timers.

Candle clocks were essentially large candles with marks down the side; the candles burned at a steady speed. The time was read from the mark below the flame.

Sand-glasses were more expensive. They were difficult to make because the hole between the two glass bulbs had to be tiny. Also, the sand inside had to be very dry in order to run smoothly from the top bulb into the lower bulb.

In a sand-glass, sand trickled slowly from the higher bulb into the lower bulb. Larger examples ran for an hour. When the hour was up, you turned the glass over to start the clock again.

HOURS LONG OR HOURS SHORT?

Our 'hour' comes from the Latin (Roman) word *hora*, but the Romans did not have regular 60-minute hours as we do today. They divided the time of daylight or darkness by 12. Summer hours were longer than winter hours, because the summer days were longer. In mid-winter the Roman day of 12 hours began at 7.30 in the morning and ended at 4.30 in the afternoon (which makes only nine of our modern hours). No-one really knew what hour it was!

KEY DATES

▶ *c.*100 BC Ctesibus of Alexandria invents a water-clock with a pointer as well as a scale

▶ *c.* AD 100 Ptolemy creates a world map; it is used in the West for more than 1,000 years

▶ *c.* AD 700 Sand-glasses in use in Western Europe

▶ *c.* AD 800 King Alfred of Wessex has candle clocks; each candle burns for four hours and each day the king sets aside eight hours (two candles) to religious matters

▶ 1070 The Chinese invent incense-burning clocks, and other 'fire clocks'; they also make huge water-powered astronomical clocks

▶ 1492 Columbus carries sand-glasses on his ships bound for the New World

ROMAN TIME

Rome made the time-rules for most of Europe and the Middle East. In 46 BC Julius Caesar modernised the calendar, and most people in the Roman empire copied it. Some 300 years later, the Roman emperor Constantine made Christianity the official religion of the empire. He made Sunday the day of rest. Previously Saturday, the Jewish Sabbath, had been the holy day for Christians and also for Roman pagans, who kept the traditional 'Saturn's day'. Constantine also made Christmas an official Christian holiday.

Constantine I (c.AD 280–337) became a Christian after seeing a vision of the cross against the Sun. He made Christianity the official religion of Rome, but the Christian or Common Era (BC and AD) dating system was not brought in until 200 years later, in AD 525.

CHURCH TIME

In the AD 300s the Christian Church began to organise the dates of its festivals. The Church wanted all Christians to celebrate festivals on the right day. Unfortunately, no dates were given in the Bible Gospels. The apostle St Paul had not bothered to date his letters to the early churches, and even scolded fellow-Christians for fussing over days and months, like pagan astrologers.

The Gospel writers agreed that Jesus had risen from the dead on the first day of the Jewish week – Sunday. But which Sunday? This was a tricky question, because it affected the date of Easter, the most important Christian festival. A meeting of Church leaders in AD 325 fixed the timing of Easter, linking it to the Jewish Moon-calendar, in use at the time Jesus was crucified.

By AD 500 the Roman empire was no more. It was now the Church in Rome which made the time-rules for Christian Europe. And so it continued for the next 1,000 years. People did not number calendar days, as we do. There were hundreds of special Saint's days in the Church calendar, so people spoke of going to market on 'St Agnes' Day', rather than '21 January'.

The Christian Church year is marked by many festivals. These people in Valencia in Spain are celebrating the feast of Saint Joseph with a parade. The clock is decorated for the occasion.

KINGS, CALENDARS AND COPERNICUS

In 1514 Pope Leo X, the head of the Catholic Church, was worried about the Church calendar being out of step with the seasons. He wrote to King Henry VIII of England, and to other kings, asking for suggestions. Henry never replied, and nothing was done. Nicolaus Copernicus, from Poland, heard about the letters. To improve the calendar, he began studying the stars and the planets. He came up with the startling suggestion that the Earth was not the centre of the Universe!

THE NUMBER PROBLEM

Throughout the Middle Ages, most people found numbers difficult to remember. They counted on their fingers, or used counting frames (abacuses) and notched 'tally sticks'. Often they made do with 'round numbers': for instance, they counted 100 rather than 104, and 200 was close enough to 189.

Roman, or Latin, numerals were still used in Europe. It was not easy to do sums using the Roman figures I, II, III, IV, V, VI, VII, VIII, IX, X and so on.

In around AD 800, a better number system appeared. It had been invented in India, and was brought to Europe by the Arabs. The new system introduced the numbers we use: 1, 2, 3, 4, 5, 6, 7, 8, 9, as well as 0. It was several hundred years before the Indian-Arabic numbers were in common use, but they made it much easier to do sums – and write dates.

Tally sticks were an ancient way of recording money transactions used in England by government tax collectors. Each notched stick was split in two down the middle, and by keeping half each, both parties (whose names were on the sticks) could keep a long-lasting record of the deal.

KEY DATES

▶ **AD 300s** The Maya of Central America may have used the zero, 500 years before its first use in Asia

▶ **AD 325** The Council of Nicaea (in what is now Turkey) fixes the date of Easter for the Christian Church

▶ **AD 476** Fall of the Roman Empire in Western Europe

▶ **AD 800** Hindu mathematicians in India develop a number system with a zero unit

▶ **1200s** The English scientist-priest, Roger Bacon, argues that people need a better system of numbers to count accurately

▶ **1400s** The zero-number system, learned from Arabs, is by now common in Europe; the first printed calendars have pictures to help people who cannot read; a black triangle means a weekday, a red triangle means a Sunday

▶ **1543** Copernicus says that the Earth travels around the Sun, and it is not the centre of the Universe (see page 18)

Making the Hours Equal

MECHANICAL TIME

By the 1200s, the medieval time-machine was creaking and the world was changing. There were new trades, such as banking; there were better machines, such as windmills and watermills; and new ideas were starting to come out of Europe's first universities. Time-keeping had to keep pace with the changes. The hours had to be made equal. Using the Sun to keep time was no longer good enough.

In the thirteenth century a European inventor (probably someone good at making mill-machinery or even toys) built the first mechanical clock. It was a wooden bell-ringing machine, driven by wheels turned by falling weights. It was a sensation.

The clock worked in the same way a bucket on a rope is drawn from a well. A weight was wound up on a long rope coiled around a drum, then released. A brake kept the rope unwinding slowly as the weight dropped. As the drum turned, so did the wheels of the 'clockwork'. One wheel moved the next as teeth, or cogs, cut around their rims fitted together. Any miller would have recognised the system.

The great iron clock in Salisbury Cathedral. Made in 1386, it is the oldest functioning clock in England. Wooden drums and weighted ropes provide the 'motor' to turn the clockwork.

BELL-RINGERS

The first clocks were set to work in churches and monasteries. They rang bells to tell the monks when it was time for services. But other clocks soon became part of town life.

The early clocks had no dials or pointers (hands). Few people could read numbers, but almost everyone could hear the clock-bells ringing the hours. Our English word 'clock' comes from the German word *Glocke* and the French *cloche* (meaning 'bell').

The earliest clocks were used in abbeys and monasteries of the Christian church. The clock-bell called the monks to their hourly services. Bells ringing the hours became part of everyday life in the Middle Ages.

In the Middle Ages, bells called people to prayers and to work, sent them to bed and woke them, warned of death and danger, and celebrated victory in war. Bells ringing the hours made people aware of time.

In 1335, the citizens of Milan in Italy marvelled at their wonderful new clock in its high bell-tower. This was the world's first public striking clock, ringing all the hours in a 24-hour day. Hearing the bells, people for the first time spoke of 'one o'clock' ('one bell of the clock') and so on, when telling the time.

▼ *The intricate astronomical clock on Prague Cathedral in the Czech Republic. Once the mechanism for the mechanical clock became widely understood, increasingly elaborate clocks and clock towers began to spring up all over Europe.*

CLOCKWATCHERS

All over Europe, people demanded a town clock. No town wanted to be without one. As clock-makers added entertaining 'extras', people came from miles around, for town clocks were now amazing public shows. Crowds gathered in town squares to watch moving mechanical figures, known as 'jacks', which appeared as if by magic on the hour, or quarter-hour, to strike the clock bells with hammers.

There were many wonderful clocks. The cathedral clock at Strasbourg in France, for example, displayed the movements of the Sun, Moon and planets. It had a calendar with the saints' days, and a tableau with moving models in which the Three Wise Men visited the Virgin Mary.

CLOCKMAKERS SHOW THEIR FACES

An Italian named Jacopo de' Dondi is said to have made the first clock with a face, or dial, in 1344. His son worked for 16 years to make one of the most complicated clocks produced in the Middle Ages. This amazing clock did not only show the time; it also showed sunrise and sunset, the days and months, and the movements of the planets. A modern copy, made from the original drawings, was built for the Smithsonian Institution in Washington, D.C.

Early on in clock history, clock dials were marked to show the quarter hours, from 1 to 4. Later this became 15, 30, 45, 60 minutes. But there were no minute hands on clocks until the seventeenth century.

A modern replica of the Dondi astronomical clock. Built in 1364 by Giovanni, son of Jacopo de' Dondi, it stands 1.5m high and shows the movement of the five planets then known.

SKILLS OF THE CLOCKMAKER

Although it might look quite straightforward by today's standards, in times past clockwork was high technology, like computers today, and clock-making was a very skilful job, involving delicate craftsmanship in wood and metal. A clockmaker hand-made each spring and screw, cut the toothed wheels and designed mechanisms such as the 'escapement' to stop the clockwork running fast or slow.

Clockmakers were masters of their craft, making intricate mechanisms by hand from brass and steel. Wooden cases for clocks became popular from the mid-seventeenth century.

Italians became particularly expert in this patient work, although there were also great French and German clockmakers. In 1540, an Italian clockmaker named Juanelo Torriano hand-cut 1,800 gear wheels on a lathe he designed himself, to make a clock for the Holy Roman Emperor, Charles V.

People were fascinated by clocks. Clockwork with its slow-turning wheels within wheels was a marvel, like God's Universe in miniature.

This Italian painting of 1558 shows a man holding a watch. As with most early watches it has only one hand. On the table is a separate alarm mechanism.

KEY DATES

▶ **1200s**	The first mechanical clocks are made in Europe
▶ **1300s**	Church and town hall clocks first ring the hours at regular intervals
▶ **1344**	The first dials appear on clocks, with hour-hands
▶ **1370**	King Charles V of France orders all clocks in France to be set to keep time by his palace clock
▶ **1386**	Salisbury Cathedral clock in England begins working; it is the oldest clock still working, even though it does not have a single screw
▶ **1400**	Italian clockmakers build the first clocks driven by springs, rather than falling weights
▶ **1480s**	The first lathe for cutting small metal screws for clocks is made in Germany
▶ **1500**	Spring-driven clocks small enough to be carried in a pocket are made by Peter Henlein in Germany
▶ **1544**	The Clockmakers' Guild is founded in Paris

Changing Times

ART AND TIME

The Renaissance, or 'rebirth', of art and learning began in Italy in the late 1300s. Artists explored the new world of perspective in painting and drawing, making pictures look three-dimensional. Artists looked at things from different angles, and at different moments in time and space. This new art changed the way people looked at the world. The ever-changing Renaissance 'cosmos' was very different from the world of perfect order in which people had believed for hundreds of years.

THE CLOCKWORK UNIVERSE

For the Ancient Greeks, and for Eastern scientists who had made important discoveries in maths and astronomy, the perfect shape was the circle or sphere. They believed that the Universe must be an arrangement of spheres. Until the 1500s, most Europeans also believed the Universe moved like the wheels inside a clock, with the Earth at its centre.

In the mid 1500s, the Polish astronomer Copernicus shocked everyone – especially the Church – by suggesting that the Sun was at the centre of this arrangement, not the Earth. Copernicus thought the sphere-system had become far too complicated. A moving Earth fitted in much more neatly with the movements of the Sun, Moon and other planets. Yet even after Copernicus, many people still liked to think of God as the 'Universal Clockmaker', maker of a perfectly harmonised universe, its secrets revealed by inventions such as the telescope and microscope.

Copernicus put the Sun at the centre on the Universe, with Earth and the other five known planets (Mercury, Venus, Mars, Saturn and Jupiter) circling around it. Beyond lay the unknown starry sphere.

CLOCKS IN CHINA

The science that was developed in China had few contacts with the West, because few foreigners visited China and few Chinese visited Europe. In 1582 Matteo Ricci, a 29-year-old missionary from Italy, arrived in China. He had come to teach Christianity, but

Matteo Ricci (1552–1610), known to the Chinese as Li Ma-tou. His knowledge of maths, maps and clocks intrigued the Chinese, who invited the missionary to Beijing to advise on a new calendar.

THE CLOCKMAKING SWISS

Switzerland is famous for clocks. The Swiss took up clockmaking in the 1700s, copying English clocks. Whole families took up the craft, making parts that were then put together by a master watchmaker. In the 1700s, it took 16 different craftsmen to make a clock and 21 to make a watch. By the 1850s, the Swiss were selling machine-made watches all over the world.

found the Chinese more interested in the clocks he brought with him. He was allowed into the Imperial Palace, but only because the emperor was keen to inspect the curious Western clocks. Being a foreigner, Ricci was not allowed to see the emperor in person.

Before Ricci brought his clocks to China, the Chinese had sucessfully kept hourly time with water-clocks, sundials and fire clocks made from slow-burning, sweet-smelling incense-sticks. By skilful use of flowing water and springs made from bamboo, the Chinese built complicated astronomical clocks to study the movements of the stars and planets.

The most famous was the Heavenly Clock, built by Su Sung. It was a wooden tower 10 m (33 ft) high, containing models of stars and planetary spheres moved by wheels turned by the force of falling water, just like watermill wheels. Every 15 minutes bells and gongs pealed, and 96 miniature figures marched to and fro.

China had produced many inventions, from paper to wheel-barrows, but the Heavenly Clock seemed clumsy alongside Father Ricci's small, intricate time-keepers. The new Western clocks entranced the emperor. More were ordered. By the 1700s the imperial palaces of China were ticking with clocks of all sizes shipped from Europe.

Su Sung's wonderful clock was a mechanical calendar, designed to mimic the movements of the stars and planets. It was completed in 1090 to aid both astronomers and astrologers, for the Chinese believed the stars influenced human lives. The picture shows a model.

KEEPING TIME

At the same time as Father Ricci was showing his clocks to the Chinese, an important discovery was being made in Italy. Watching a lamp swing from a chain inside a church, a bright young scientist named Galileo Galilei saw to his surprise that each swing lasted the same time. He had discovered the laws of the pendulum.

Because its motion was so regular, a pendulum could make a clock keep near-perfect time. In 1657, the Dutch scientist Christiaan Huygens designed the first pendulum clock, which made the old weight-driven clocks look immediately out-of-date. Clockmaking was becoming a science.

The new clocks had more complicated workings inside. Catching levers called escapements kept the pendulum swinging steadily. As the small toothed wheels of the clock clicked together, the clock made the 'tick-tock' sound that was to become familiar in homes all over the world in the next 200 years.

SPRING TIME

Springs, as well as weights, had long been used to make clockwork toys, and by 1600 spring clocks were becoming popular. A coiled metal main-spring provided the 'engine' for the clockwork.

A wound-up spring stores energy, which is released as the spring unwinds. The more the spring unwinds, the less energy it has, so the clock begins to run slow even before it needs rewinding. To solve this problem, clockmakers took an idea from gunsmiths – a cone-shaped spool called a fusee, to give extra 'drive' to the weakening spring.

Spring clocks could be made small enough to go inside decorative cases. Some were very strange. There were egg-shaped clocks, clocks inside wooden birds and even clocks in human skulls! Most clocks still looked better than they worked. Even with the improvements, no two clocks in a house kept the same time for long.

A pendulum clock made in 1753 for the French king Louis XV. The swinging pendulum kept the clock in time. Clockmakers found that a pendulum 1 m(3 ft) long would swing once a second.

BALANCED TIMEKEEPING

An ingenious Englishman named Robert Hooke, who lived in the seventeenth century, built his first clock out of wood, having watched a clock being taken to pieces. Hooke later invented the balance spring which kept the clockwork running more smoothly and therefore helped the clock keep better time. To Hooke's annoyance, Huygens had the same idea, and the latter got the credit for making the first balance-spring watch in 1674.

Christiaan Huygens looks proudly at his new pendulum clock of 1657, in the shop of clockmaker Salomon Coster.

GETTING UP WITH THE CLOCK

Time had moved from the bell-tower to the mantelpiece and into people's pockets. Men carried watches on chains, tucked away in waistcoat pockets. Women kept them in their bags. Glancing at the clock indoors was becoming daily routine. People got up and came home from work by clock time, not by the Sun.

A gold watch and chain, a royal present given to the Scottish surgeon Matthew Baillie in 1811.

MAKING SENSE OF THE UNIVERSE

In the meantime, the Universe was proving a more complicated clock than any-one thought. The German astronomer, Johannes Kepler, had shown in the early 1600s that the planets moved around the Sun in ellipses (ovals), not circles. The closer to the Sun a planet moved, the faster it travelled.

Like scientists before him, Kepler still likened the 'celestial machine' to a clock. But it was a clock that seemed to move at varying speeds. A new mathematics was needed to make sense of the baffling new ideas about time and motion.

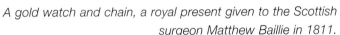

KEY DATES

▶ **1583**   Galileo realises that a swinging pendulum can keep time
▶ **1657**   Christiaan Huygens of the Netherlands designs the first pendulum clock
▶ **1670**   Minute hands are now common on clocks; William Clement of England makes a long pendulum; this leads to the appearance of the long-case or grandfather clock.
▶ **1670s** The balance spring makes clocks much more accurate, by controlling oscillation (vibration)

The New Universe

A NEW WORLD

In the age of Isaac Newton (1642–1727), science progressed rapidly through experiment, observation and precise measurement of time. There was also an amazing space sensation: in 1758 Halley's Comet (as it is known today) blazed across the skies. It had last been seen in 1682. Edmond Halley had predicted the comet's reappearance. Its return – at the time Halley had predicted – seemed to show that there was regular time-keeping in the Universe.

Newton was the greatest scientist of his day. He put forward a set of principles, or laws, to explain the forces that move the Earth and Universe – his laws showed why the planets travel around the Sun, and why an apple falls to the ground. Newton's work set the scientific clock ticking faster.

Isaac Newton spent his old age trying to use his knowledge of astronomy to fix dates in the Bible and history, and so draw up a 'worldwide time line'.

THE TIMETABLING PROBLEM

The industrial clock was ticking even more rapidly. In the 1700s came the first steam engines and the start of the factory age. By the 1830s railway travel had become more common and further problems appeared. Drawing up timetables for train passengers was very difficult, because there was no standard time: different parts of the country kept their own time. Clocks on railway stations showed both 'railway time' (the train company's time) and local time. This was very confusing for passengers. The age of fast train travel demanded one time for all.

The Royal Greenwich Observatory near London had become the authority on timekeeping. Its telescopes and clocks were the most accurate in the world. In 1880, all the railways in Britain switched to Greenwich Time.

 The Royal Observatory at Greenwich was founded in 1675 by King Charles II to improve star-watching, time-keeping and navigation.

INTERNATIONAL TIME

Trains ran across Europe from one country to another, and by the 1880s tracks also stretched huge distances across North and South America, Africa and Asia. World railways, and world trade, needed a common time to avoid confusion. With the invention in 1876 of the telephone, which allowed people to talk one-to-one over many miles for the first time, the time problem became more serious. It was clear that countries, as well as train stations, must agree on clock-time.

In 1884, experts from the leading nations met in Washington, D.C., in the U.S., and agreed to make Greenwich Mean Time the standard against which time around the world was set. The Washington conference set up 24 time zones, which we still have today.

TIME RULES

In the industrialised world, time was now master. Factories had fixed working hours, set by law. Children went to school at set times. Shops advertised 'opening hours'.

Public clocks were everywhere, in streets and squares, to make sure that everyone knew the time. People had clocks in their homes and watches in their pockets. By 1914, many people never went out without a wrist-watch, which were first worn by women.

Town meetings and entertainment began and ended at set times. With a watch in hand, people were able to time the fastest runners in races, fix the periods of play in football matches, and keep records such as noting the daily temperature at regular times.

John Harwood developed the first self-winding wristwatch in the 1920s, although self-winding mechanisms were applied to pocket watches as early as the eighteenth century.

KEY DATES

▶ **1687** Newton's ideas about gravitation and the laws of motion are published

▶ **1840** The first battery-powered clock is invented, although it still has a spring and pendulum

▶ **1862** Greenwich Observatory sends an hourly time signal by telegraph to Big Ben (London's most famous public clock, named after the bell in its tower).

▶ **1869** Charles Dowd proposes 'time zones' in the U.S.A.. U.S. and Canadian railroads adopt time zones in 1883

▶ **1884** Greenwich Mean Time becomes the international standard time

▶ **1890** Wrist-watches become popular, soon replacing pocket watches

▶ **1906** The first all-electric clock is invented

▶ **1924** British Broadcasting Corporation (BBC) begins broadcasting time signals as 'pips'

▶ **1929** The first quartz crystal clock is invented at Bell Laboratories in the U.S.; most modern clocks and watches use the quartz crystal system

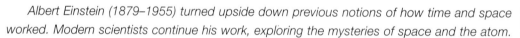

Time and Space

RELATIVE TIME

Can we measure time just as we measure a piece of string? The answer is a bit more complicated than that. Until the beginning of the twentieth century most people believed in 'absolute' time, where time 'happened' at the same instant everywhere, for example a clock on a station and another clock on a train speeding through the station must show the same time.

In everyday life this is true. But what if the train was travelling at a speed close to the speed of light (a little under 300,000 km per second)? Thinking about how time and speed were related, in 1905 the German-born scientist Albert Einstein came up with a new theory, about 'relativity'.

Einstein suggested that there was no absolute (fixed) time. If a train could travel at near light speed (300,000 km/sec), then a clock on the train will seem, to someone on a station, to run slow. While the clock on the train might show that six seconds had passed, the person looking at the station clock would see that ten seconds had passed. This theory made scientists think again, but has not yet affected our daily lives, lived at 'normal' speed.

Space (a box, for example) has three dimensions: length, width and height. Einstein added a fourth dimension: time.

Albert Einstein (1879–1955) turned upside down previous notions of how time and space worked. Modern scientists continue his work, exploring the mysteries of space and the atom. ▲

ATOMIC CLOCKS

Many old wind-up clocks lose or gain minutes each week. We seldom have to put our modern clocks or watches right. A modern quartz crystal clock loses or gains only one second every 10 years, so regular is the frequency of the vibrating crystal inside.

Atomic clocks are even more accurate. An atomic clock controlled by a beam of caesium atoms will lose only one second in one million years! There are now several thousand atomic clocks – some in satellites in

 Caesium clocks like these at the UK's National Physical Laboratory are used to set all other timing systems.

TIME CAPSULES

During the twentieth century, people buried ' time capsules', to amuse or inform future generations. A typical capsule contains a selection of items from our time, which will hopefully be dug up and looked at in the future. Most capsules contain small items such as clothes, letters, photographs, music tapes and bars of chocolate.

space, sending time signals to aid navigation and communications on Earth. These super-accurate clocks also control radio time signals and 'talking clock' services provided by phone companies.

SPACE-TIME TRAVEL

Time behaves oddly when objects speed up. Nothing can travel faster than light – about 300,000 km per second (186,000 miles per second). If astronauts could travel at a speed approaching the speed of light, time in their spacecraft would slow down. They would age more slowly than people left behind on Earth.

Astronauts returning from a space trip at near-light speed could find their children were older than they were! For now such weird possibilities remain in the realms of science fiction.

Astronauts during the Moon landings of 1969–72 were still in the same time-frame as Earth. Beyond the Solar System, communication will take longer and time might start to play tricks on future space explorers.

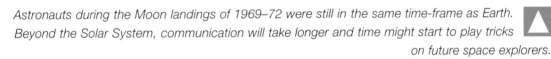

KEY DATES

▶ **1675**   Ole Romer of Denmark measures the speed of light by timing eclipses of the moons of the planet Jupiter

▶ **1887**   In America, Albert Michelson and Edward Morley prove by experiment that the speed of light is always the same

▶ **1904**   Time signals are first broadcast by radio

▶ **1905**   Einstein publishes a paper on his special theory of relativity

▶ **1955**   The world's first caesium-beam atomic clock begins keeping time in England

▶ **1960**   U.S. scientists Robert Pound and Glen Rebka confirm Einstein's theory of 'relative time' by measuring the behaviour of photons (particles of radiation).

▶ **1971**   By flying atomic clocks around the world in jet planes, U.S. scientists J. C. Hafele and R. E. Keating show that time can indeed run at different speeds

▶ **1998**   On 31 December, there is a 61-second minute, to let the Earth catch up with atomic clock time (tides tend to slow down the Earth's spin)

Living Time

NATURAL CLOCKS

Nature has its own time systems. Plants and animals have their own 'body clocks'. In animals, body clocks control the timing of important activities such as migration, feeding and breeding. Body clocks tell the animal when it is time to do these things.

Some natural clocks tick away for years, then suddenly ring, like an alarm. An insect called the 17-year cicada spends the first 17 years of its life underground.

Then its clock tells it that it's time to go, and it digs itself out, changing from a grub to a winged adult insect.

Animals' clocks respond to changes in the seasons. Animals that hibernate, such as ground squirrels, react to the approach of winter by 'shutting down' and going into a deep sleep. While hibernating, their body clocks run very slowly, conserving energy.

▲ *Migrating animals like these African wildebeest make long seasonal journeys. Many migrants seem to have an inborn 'calendar' that tells them when to migrate, and their own navigation systems for finding the way.*

OBEYING INSTINCT

Shoreline and seabed creatures move and feed to the rhythms of the ocean tides. The Moon is their clock. Grunion, small ocean fishes, swim on to California's beaches shortly after the full moon, to lay their eggs at the high tide. In laboratory tests, sea anemones kept to the same feeding rhythms, even when moved in tanks far from the seashore. They still obeyed the pull of the Moon, which causes the tides.

Animals can be trained to do things at the same time every time. In 1912 a Russian researcher named Ivan Pavlov fed dogs every 30 minutes. The dogs' mouths would water, anticipating food, every half-hour – even if no food was there. Many other animals feed at the same times every day, and even bees have been trained to come for food at regular intervals.

▶ *Marine turtles return to the same beaches to lay their eggs at the same time every year, obeying the call of the Moon and tides.*

LIFE AND DEATH

Unlike plants and animals, people know that death ends life. We know that time is passing. We age and we see and feel the changes that happen to our bodies. What happens after life is a key teaching of the great religions. Christianity and Islam teach that death is followed by a new life in heaven. In Buddhism and Hinduism, the belief is that people are born and reborn many times.

▲ *The oceans have a regular rhythm of life, to which creatures like these sea anemones feed and spawn. Many fish swim up to the surface to feed at night, when they are safer from predators.*

SUSPENDED ANIMATION

For some living things, time appears to stand still. They can look dead, but can return to life after years of 'suspended animation'.

A wheat seed dropped by a slave in an Egyptian tomb 4,000 years ago may sprout and grow, if brought into the light and given water. Small animals called rotifers can be dried or frozen, but come back to life in a teaspoon of water. Bacteria entombed in rock for millions of years stir and begin multiplying if released into favourable conditions.

HOW TIME PASSES

Humans have body clocks too. For example, many of us wake up at roughly the same time each morning. Flying across time zones in fast jets can confuse our bodies – this is known as 'jet lag'.

We lose track of time if we cannot see daylight and have no clocks. People kept in darkened rooms become confused about the passage of time. One volunteer researcher, who was shut in for 58 days, thought that only 33 days had passed. Time seems to drag if we are bored. Yet time passes too quickly when we are enjoying ourselves.

Past, Present and Future

ARCHEOLOGICAL TIME

People who explore the past – archeologists – want to know how old objects are. One way is radiocarbon dating. Living things take in carbon from food and air, and part of that carbon is a radioactive form called carbon-14. It decays (breaks down and disappears) at a known rate – half the carbon-14 disappears after about 5,730 years. By measuring how much carbon-14 is left in a piece of wood, wood or bone archeologists can work out how old it is. Radiocarbon 'clocks' can be checked by counting tree rings (trees add one growth ring every year).

The science of archeology began in the 1800s. Since then there have been finds like the 4,000-year-old treasures of Troy and the terracotta warriors of ancient China. Time-measuring helps us to explore the past, so much so that computers can recreate lost cities in virtual reality. The clues time gives us are few, and the evidence sometimes puzzling. Yet often we discover that people who lived thousands of years ago were just like us.

GOING ROUND IN CYCLES?

The Greeks and other peoples of the ancient world believed that time moved in cycles. Civilisations rose and fell – it seemed as if there was no beginning and no end to time. Jews, Christians and Muslims, however, believe that time is a line, with a beginning (a Creator-God) and progress towards an end – the end of the world.

WHAT KIND OF FUTURE?

From the 1700s, revolutions in industry and science convinced many people in Europe and America that time would make people 'better' (more civilised). The idea of 'progress' came to dominate Western life, and spread almost everywhere. Science seemed to offer a future with more of every-thing – cars, televisions, washing machines, computers – the list seemed endless.

▲ *Terracotta warriors discovered in Xian, China in 1974. An estimated 8,000 figures including cavalrymen and charioteers guard the nearby and still unopened tomb of China's first emperor, Qin Shihvang.*

But is more of everything, for everyone, possible? Or even desirable? As we look ahead into this twenty-first century, many people are not so certain. It is not easy to predict what life will be like in 100 years, let alone in 500 or 1,000 years time.

Cities change constantly. In 1800 Singapore was a swampy island. Now skyscrapers dwarf the few old nineteenth-century buildings that remain.

TIME TRAVEL

We cannot go forward to see what the future will bring. Time travel remains only a dream. Fantasy film-makers show us what the future could be like in TV shows and movies such as *Star Trek* and *Star Wars*.

In an early science fiction story, the British writer H. G. Wells sent his hero off in a time machine. If such a machine were possible, what would you do? Would you travel back in time to your favourite period of history? Or would you leap into the future?

The crew of Star Trek crew 'warped' their way between galaxies at incredible speed, and occasionally slipped through time. In real life, we are confined to here and now, at least for the present.

KEY DATES

▶ **1600s** The first modern statistics, when John Graunt studies population, disease and death rates from local records in London

▶ **1790** The U.S. is the first country to organise a national census, or population count, now held every 10 years

▶ *c.* **1815** Christian Thomsen of Denmark organises museum exhibits into groups – stone, bronze and iron; these are the 'Three Ages' used ever since by most history writers

▶ **1800s** The discovery of dinosaur fossils and a new understanding of rock strata leads to the division of geological time, into periods, epochs and eras

▶ **1895** H. G. Wells publishes his story of time travel, *The Time Machine*

▶ **1928** *Amazing Stories* is America's first science fiction magazine

▶ **1940s** Radiocarbon dating is developed by American chemist Willard E. Libby and his colleagues, for dating objects aged between 500 and 50,000 years

▶ **1958** Scientists make atomic clocks the standard for defining world time units, such as the second

Glossary

Archeology
The study of the past through excavation of sites, such as tombs and settlements, and discovery of old objects.

Astrologer
A person who believes the stars and planets shape our personalities and our future lives.

Astronomer
A scientist who studies the stars and planets through observation.

Atomic Clocks
The most accurate clocks yet made; they count the electromagnetic waves given off or absorbed by atoms of caesium, hydrogen or ammonia.

Balance Spring
A spring that coils and uncoils to regulate the timekeeping of a clock.

Calendar
A chart or table showing the days, weeks and months of the year.

Comet
A ball of ice and dust which travels around the Sun, trailing a long tail.

Cycle
A series of events which are repeated in the same order.

Day
The time from sunrise to sunset; it can also mean the 24-hour period from midnight to midnight.

Degree
A unit of measurement (temperature or the angle of a circle, for example). A circle has 360 degrees.

Dial
The face of a clock, originally the face of a sundial.

Digital Clocks
Clocks that show the time in digits (such as 14.23) in a display panel.

Dinosaur
A group of reptiles, now extinct. The name means 'terrible lizard'.

Eclipse
The blocking of light from the Sun or the Moon. The Moon may pass between the Earth and the Sun (solar eclipse), or the Earth may block sunlight from reaching the Moon (lunar eclipse). Eclipses were startling events in ancient times.

Escapement
A device in a clock which regulates the movement of the pendulum or gear wheels.

Festival
A special time of holiday or religious celebration.

Fossil
The remains of a long-dead animal or plant, preserved in rock.

Gear Wheels
Toothed wheels arranged so that one moves the next; in clocks, a series of linked wheels is called a train.

Jesus Christ
In Christianity, the Son of God; his teachings are the basis for the Christian faith.

Latin
The language of the Ancient Romans, later used by the Church in Europe and by scholars.

Main-spring
The spring inside a clock that is wound up by turning a key; as it uncoils, it drives the clock.

Mesopotamia
The land between the rivers Tigris and Euphrates (modern Iraq), home of several important early civilisations.

Millennium
A period of 1,000 years, from the Latin *mille* (1,000) and *annus* (year).

Month
A twelfth part of a year, with 30 or 31 days. February has 28 days except in a leap-year, when it has 29.

Nile
The longest river in the world, flowing from central Africa northwards through Egypt into the Mediterranean Sea.

Orbit
The path followed by a moon or planet as it moves around another body in space. The Moon orbits the Earth, and the Earth orbits the Sun.

Migration
Seasonal journeys made by some animals, especially birds.

Pendulum
A weighted metal rod that swings at a regular rate; in pendulum clocks, altering the position of the weight, or bob, makes the pendulum swing faster or slower – and so makes the clock run faster or slower.

Planet
A large body in space orbiting a star.

Pope
The head of the Roman Catholic Church.

Quartz
A mineral; tiny quartz crystals are kept vibrating in clocks and watches.

Renaissance
A period of 'rebirth' of learning in Western Europe, affecting art and science, that began in the 1300s.

Roman Catholic Church
The largest and oldest of the Christian churches, with its headquarters in Rome.

Romans
Ancient people who ruled an empire that grew from Italy to control much of Europe, North Africa and the Near East until its collapse in the AD 400s.

Sand-glass
An early clock, in which sand trickled from one glass bulb into another very slowly, measuring time

Seasons
Part of the year; such as the four seasons of cool countries (spring, summer, autumn, winter).

Solar
Means 'of the Sun'.

Solstice
The moment each year when the Sun is either at its most northerly (the shortest day) or most southerly position (the longest day); the winter solstice in the northern half of the world is about 21 December, the summer solstice is about 21 June.

Star
A huge ball of hot gas in space, giving off energy as light; the Sun is a medium-sized star.

Sun
The star around which the nine planets of our Solar System move in orbit.

Universe
Everything that exists in space, including all the stars and other matter in it.

Year
The time it takes for the Earth to make one orbit around the Sun; our calendar year is made up of 365 days. Years on other planets are longer or shorter.

Index